LIFE ON THE EDGE
OF THE CONTINENT

SELECTED POEMS OF
RONALD KOERTGE

THE UNIVERSITY OF ARKANSAS PRESS

FAYETTEVILLE, 1982

Library of Congress Cataloging in Publication Data

    Koertge, Ronald.
      Life on the edge of the continent.

     I. Title.
    PS3561.0347L5   811′.54   81–13094
    ISBN 0–938626–04–3   AACR2
    ISBN 0–938626–05–1 (pbk.)

Acknowledgments

Most of the poems in this volume have been previously published in periodicals. "A Jockey," "Royce Newport Money," "A Man like a Curtain," "Waiting," "Two Men," "Old People," "The Ubiquity of the Need for Love," "Sex Object," and "Streetsweeper" were first published in *Sex Object*, copyright © 1977 by the Country Press. "I Wanted My Name on the Side of a Building I Wanted to Be as Feared as the Word Biopsy," "For My Daughter," "The Quiz," "The Day Alvero Pineda Was Killed," and "Life on the Edge of the Continent" were first published in *Men Under Fire* by Duck Down Press. "A Jockey," "A Man like a Curtain," "Waiting," "Two Men," "Old People," "The Ubiquity of the Need for Love," "Sex Object," "Gretel," "Mr. Big," "Sidekicks," "Urban Renewal," "The Caboose Factory," "Panty Hose," "Excerpts from God's Secret Diary," "Pronouncing My Name," "Whippersnappers," "Last-Minute Change of Plans," "These Students Couldn't Write Their Way out of a Paper Bag," "Night Games,"and "Sleep" are reprinted by permission of Little Caesar Press. *The Father Poems* is reprinted by permission of Sumac Press. "Orientation Week," "To Impress the Girl Next Door," and "My Grandmother" appeared in *Twelve Photographs of Yellowstone* by Red Hill Press. "Reading at the Local High School," "In South America on Business He Does Something He Is Ashamed of yet on the Way Home Dreams of It Again and Again," and "Primary Considerations" are reprinted by permission of *The Wormwood Review*. Grateful acknowledgment is also made to *Maelstrom Review* and *Mid-Atlantic Review*.

Contents

PRIMARY CONSIDERATIONS

Simon calls. It seems his new
wife is having an affair with
Richard.

I try to console him: "How
serious can it be? After all,
Dick and Jane."

He is scornful. "Don't be simple
minded. Remember Jill? That
sounded innocent too, but I got
the kids and people are still
talking about what went on
up there."

said she didn't know anything about ovens
so the witch crawled in to show her
and Bam! went the big door.

Then she strolled out to the shed where
her brother was fattening, knocked down
a wall and lifted him high in the air.

Not long after the adventure in the forest
Gretel married so she could live happily.
Her husband was soft as Hansel. Her
husband liked to eat. He liked to see
her in the oven with the pies and cakes.

Ever after was the size of a kitchen.
Gretel remembered when times were better.
She laughed out loud when the witch
popped like a weenie.

"Gretel! Stop fooling around and fix
my dinner."

"There's something wrong with this oven,"
she says, her eyes bright as treasure.
"Can you come here a minute?"

Every heavy in every afternoon
movie wanted to see
him.

And no wonder. Who doesn't have
an idea that only Mr. Big
can handle.

Yet waiting, turning your hat
in your hands, whom do you see?
Mr. Little.

That's why people are religious,
because there's a chance of finally
seeing Him

smoking the entire state of Florida.

They were never handsome and often came
with a hormone imbalance manifested by corpulence,
a yodel of a voice or ears big as kidneys.

But each was brave. More than once a sidekick
has thrown himself in front of our hero in order
to receive the bullet or blow meant for that
perfect face and body.

Thankfully, heroes never die in movies and leave
the sidekick alone. He would not stand for it.
Gabby or Pat, Pancho or Andy remind us of a part
of ourselves,

the dependent part that can never grow up,
the part that is painfully eager to please,
always wants a hug and never gets enough.

Who could sit in a darkened theatre, listen
to the organ music and watch the best
of ourselves lowered into the ground while
the rest stood up there, tears pouring off
that enormous nose.

named Kovacs went down
at Pomona yesterday.
He was riding something
that was born to hold
one piece of paper
to another.

The crowd loves to hate
accidents and everybody
wanted to know who Ted
Kovacs was. Like the
next winner, it was
a mystery.

This, then, is to set
the record straight:
Ted Kovacs makes 14
thousand a year when
things go right.

His wife keeps a
scrapbook that shows
the day he tripled,
the $9000.00 Exacta
where he was second,
and all the times he
was in intensive care.

When he almost didn't make it,
the article ran to nearly
20 lines.

The Day Alvero Pineda Was Killed

It was almost post time, the horses were
lining up. Pineda's was spooking so he
stepped off, outguessing trouble, and stood
on a little shelf in the stall of the
Puett starting gate.

Nobody knows what happened, but people
with binoculars saw the sudden blood. They
stared as if he had removed his helmet
to reveal a fall of thick, red hair.

The siren faded, the race went off, somebody
won. Then the announcement that he was
dead. "Boots and Saddles," a moment
of silence.

For the rest of the day we worked
the bartenders numb and heaved our money
through the windows, making everything
the favorite.

After the ninth we went home
38,000 of us
all sick
all broke

feeling lucky.

had everything including monogrammed
    sandwiches
but after graduation he refused to go into
    business
with his father. He wanted to get out on his own,
see where his head was at and find out if there
    wasn't
more to life than getting and spending.

No, Royce did not want to be carried on his
    quest by
faithful servants. He wanted to hitchhike.

A grizzled old farmer gave him his first lift. He
    was
a man whose father had lost everything in the
    Dust Bowl
and he himself had eaten an anthill, but he said
    he
wouldn't trade places with Howard Hughes.

A madam on the skids took him as far as
    Collinsville.
Hell, she'd been through as many fortunes as
    there are
days in the week and between the good times took
    second
billing in a stag smoker act named "Raoul & The
Swine Woman."
But she was happy, yes sir!

Outside of Waco he met a gambler, a man who
    had never
won a bet in his life. He was sitting in the back
of a truck stop because he'd lost his clothes
    betting
that a mummy would be next out of the rest room
    at the
House of Pies. Was he happy? As a clam.

It was like that clear across the country and back:
    poor
but happy, salt of the earth, laugh and let
    the world
go by.

At home Royce crowed to his father, who smiled
    and pushed
a button to reveal them all, a cast of thousands
with his money in their sweaty hands.

Royce was crushed. He wanted to kill himself and
    be
buried in potter's field. His dad gave him a
    platinum
gun with his name on it, then showed a film of his
    funeral,
a get-together that made "The Feast of Paradise"
    look like
a Kappa Sig beer blast.

Royce sighed, picked up a pen, and got down to
    work.

The lady on the corner is out in the woodlot
behind her house. I can see her from an
upper window. Clumsy in her winter clothes,
she smashes branch against heavy branch.

The unhappy sound seems to unhinge the
neighborhood because when the other women
walk their dogs or daughters in the evening
all they can talk about is WHY? And

when they meet, they reveal the nature of
their own fears. "Malignancy," says one.
"She is childless,"croons another. "Mad,"
says still a third, while the only Christian

maintains that any sort of exercise is
better than none at all.

I do not know why the lady on the corner is
out in the woodlot behind her house, but
certainly she is there: arms raised like
Lizzie Borden, she staggers, drunken-

lumberjack, from the exertion of every blow.
She has been at it for hours, and the
bruised wood is piled around her feet like
a pyre while on her face she wears the

look of colossal disappointment that
is sometimes seen in the expressions
of aging ladies who have just been told
that they have fifty years to live.

goes by at 1:00 a.m. two nights of the week. I can
hear the feather whoosh of his machine and see
one red light.

I believe that the streetsweeper lives alone,
    sleeping
through the cold days, waking clear-eyed and deft
as the sun goes down.

I believe that he works steadily without a portable
radio or a reading light or a nap. When he pauses
it is to stare placidly into
the potent night.

For reasons too numerous to mention, I think
    about the
streetsweeper often and about the singular,
    provident
cadence of his life.

In South America on Business He Does Something He Is Ashamed of yet on the Way Home Dreams of It Again and Again

He liked the whores in Guatemala
City. He liked their coloring books
and dirty feet. When he paid,
the American dollars shook like
leaves.

The stewardess wakes him again,
"It's just a dream," she says.
He sees décolletage. He looks
away: not that, not now. Too
close to home, the wife, the
little girl.

Urban Renewal

A man decides to exercise regularly and build up his body. He starts very, very carefully, merely standing on the edge of the sagging stairs and stretching the Achilles tendons. While he feels just the same, little by little the stairs look better. Push-ups? By May the slanting floor had evened out and the bald spots in the rug had sprouted new shag. Probably isometric exercises in all the doorways will put the whole place back on even keel. Sure enough. The place turns into a Showcase House and is just about to get the local Improvement Award when the cops show up and nab the man for building without a permit. Hiding their grins behind their hats, they hurry him off to the rotting, decrepit jail.

woke up one morning with a stone tied to his
tongue. He could no longer kiss nor speak
without disgust or derision. He was in
despair and more than once thought about
folding himself away for good.

But women as tall and beautiful as masts began
to look at him and run their tongues around
their lips as if they had just inherited
hot butterscotch sundaes

and men who had previously thought of him
as 9:40 a.m. suddenly put their arms around
his shoulders until they were stacked up
like bananas.

Then one morning the stone was gone. Piled
at the foot of his bed like Russian quilts
were women deprived of lips for the first
time. Crouched by the lamps were men who
had never heard another human be silent.

"Everything's okay now," the man said, "let's
have breakfast."
"Fake," said the women, getting up and shaking
themselves flat as towels, "you're no G. Cooper."
"Breakfast," said the men, "and we thought
you were measured and grave."

Alone, he tried to attach a stone to his
tongue but could not. He was still trying
when a breeze blew through his apartment
and lifted him parallel to the floor.

The Burglar

He was too good, that's why he never got anywhere.
At his first job as a fry cook, he either baked
everything into oblivion or spent so much time
arranging it attractively that it got cold and
hard. When an angry patron sailed a fried egg at
him and it stuck in the wall, he quit.

A month later he found work in a veterinary's
office. His first assignment was to wash a Great
Dane. When he finished the dog was half-dead and
mad with pain.

Frustrated, he decided to turn to crime and get
revenge on a world he never made. Things haven't
improved:

Every night he goes out, the aluminum ladder
clanking against the saw, his metal safety hat
forever dropping off as he bends to retrieve the
jars and cans, bottles and tins that tumble
from his pockets.

Behind him, the houses light up in sleepy succession:
"What the hell was that?" ask the owners. "Christ,
I never heard such a racket."

While outside he walks, a hundred dogs yapping at
his heels, metal-soled climbing shoes grating on
the pavement, eyes fixed on the quiet houses
at the end of the block.

It'd been twenty minutes at least
and walking around the booth,
smoking, looking into the gutter,
leaning, I'd overheard parts of

every conversation and there had
been a lot: his roll of dimes
was drooping.

"Hello, Mabel? Say, why don't you
and I . . ." and then I'd wander off
and check my life line.

"Marge? Is this old Marge the senior
class cutup?" Hunkering down I
inspected the gravel and filters.

"Ethel? Ethel, you probably don't
remember me, but . . ." I started to
count red Fords.

When the door finally opened, I was
ready but he only threw out the
green coin tube, crumpled.

I sighed. He dialed. "Hello, Mom?"
There wasn't any seat but he kind
of sat down anyway. He was rubbing
his head where the hair used to be.

"It's Richie, Mom, remember? I was
the baby of the family."

I hailed a cab and told the guy
to step on it.

The Quiz

A couple we know were into everything:
astrology, organic foods, heavy drugs,
pendulums, tarot, subsistence, cycling,
the revolution, the movement, awareness,
self-hypnosis, alpha waves, macrame,
fasting, automatic writing, zen.

Younger than us, cooler, I never saw
them hold hands or pay much
attention to each other.

They got married last weekend and this
morning when he started his new job
she walked out to the car and kissed
him goodbye.

True or False:
This is a step in the right
direction.

and a family of two is exploring the Student Union.
Dad is all decked out in the shirt she bought with
her own money. Joyce is wearing snug cutoffs and
her freshman breasts stir as she walks.

Dad knows that all the boys plan to slip some LSD
in her cocoa as soon as he is out of sight. He
takes in the monsters, their hair down to there,
a fuselage in every pair of pants.

Worse than he expected, certainly not the eunuchs
and mild wethers that he hoped for. And where is
The Jake Barnes Dormitory?

He sees them do it to her even as they stand by the
car. Worse, he sees her ask for it, coaxing with
her expensive teeth. Why can't he
lock those vivid hips in her room?
Follow her everywhere, revolvers drawn?
Punch a few of those furry bastards in the chops?

So he does what he can—lips to chaste brow, hand
to bare arm saying,

Good-by now. Be good.

The Zenith and After

He was sitting in front of the fire, looking out
the big picture window and watching the deer browse
on the short green grass that grew up through the
snow. In the other room his beautiful children were
playing quietly.

He sipped his drink and breathed a huge sigh of
   contentment.

When he heard a woman's laughter, he walked to the
   front
door and looked out. There he saw his wife sprawled
in the back seat of the station wagon. Except for one
tennis shoe she was nude.

Starting at the door on the driver's side and leading
down the driveway for a few yards was a short line
of men:
two college kids in fraternity sweatshirts, one short
man with a Corsican bandit's mustache, one
   Episcopalian
minister, and an ice cream man sucking on a popsicle.
All of them had their pants down around their ankles
and were chatting amiably.

When he he heard his children start to scream he
   turned,
and as he sprinted through the living room
he noticed that the deer were gone, too.

On a certain part of the lawn outside the
college at the edge of town, the common
student comes to love.

You never see the campus queens out there
or the pouty-looking owners of Corvettes,

only the under-achievers, the ones who
take the bus everywhere
and live at home.

Between classes they lie in the sun,
carbuncle to carbuncle
glasses folded and put away
their bad breath mingling like a
successful experiment in Chem. II
while twenty miles away, on the shore of
the blue Pacific, the head cheerleader and
secretary of the freshman class

pulls her short skirt back into place and
says

Not here, Tom,
not now.

The Caboose Factory

10,000 men
on the
pasadena
freeway
all in
love
with
the
word
    drifter

and two women were racing. Sometimes
a man won, sometimes a woman.

In the course of this event, the contestants
grew fond of one another. The men
were ashamed of themselves, however,
and each chose a wife.

Now the teams raced. Sometimes one team
won, sometimes the other.

"Let's make this more interesting,"
said the men and they gave one of the women
a Norge and a Hoover and a Singer to carry.
The other had to hold a baby and every
so often douche or shave her legs without
stopping and without putting down the baby.
Sometimes one of the women won, sometimes
the other.

"Let's get in on this," said the men
and they sprinted to the wire, looking back
over their shoulders and laughing.

"It's all over," they said, "we won."
But the women kept on
coming.

Panty Hose

A little after 5:00 the curb in front of
the Bank of America is rich with typists
holding their cold elbows and waiting for
boys who are pale and hairy, who play a
little guitar, always have some good dope
and do not work.

These girls in their panty hose are sowing
their wild oats now because soon each will
leave the hair and the ribs-that-show
for their legacy, the movie Mom ran every
day of their lives.

Already they hate their husbands for sucking
up to big shots, for voting Republican
and pointing out creeps in vans. They will
never love anybody like they do the one
who is always late. They will never look
up and down the street so eagerly, not
even when dinner is ice-cold and someone
in a new Country Squire has just been
involved in a terrible crash.

were disappearing left and right, so the police came.
"Description of the missing person?"
"Well, he was old . . . "
"You fit the description. Case closed."

More failed to show for checkers. Benches stood idle as ribs. A few good sons called up. "I hate to bother you, sergeant, but you know how it is when you dad's been gone for six or seven months."

Two go-gettum rookies were assigned to the case. They stood around in regulation mufti scaring penny ante dealers.

Then while an old guy was waiting for a light, a Chevy van pulled up. On the green, nothing. They followed, collared the driver beside a warehouse, wrung the truth out of him:

He was an orphan; he had been snatching senior citizens off the streets then hugging and kissing them for days. All cancelled their doctors' appointments, some ran off with each other, a few died from happiness.

At the arraignment thousands of old folks surged around the courthouse. They threw catheters, bifocals and trusses at the helmeted cops.

"Me next, me next," they shouted so loud and fierce that they drowned out the sirens closing in from everywhere.

Eve has just succumbed to the serpent. He is quite handsome. If I say so myself, I make a good snake. Now Eve is about to feel desire. How odd to invent it then be without it, like Thomas Edison in the dark.

Now they've really done it. Each gets an A for contrition, but out they go anyway. I must remember to remove the angel with the flaming sword. If he stays there until Los Angeles appears, people will think this is a car wash.

Today I am ambivalent about these particular manifestations of my self. It won't be long before there will be commandments and pathological introspection. On the other hand, I am a sucker for sweet talk. Already Eve is a spellbinder. She is so cute on her knees that I want to answer all her prayers.

It is Saturday night on Earth. Adam & Eve are restless—perhaps dread of Sunday and reminders of what their shenanigans cost them. Perhaps it is just the weekend and they are already fun's hostage.

I can hear anything in any cosmos and beyond, yet I choose the sound of their troubled hearts. What a funny God I am.

THE FATHER POEMS

He

had a bay stallion once that the Triple Bar C
gave him to ride herd with, and it was a big
awkward thing. He could never trust it
in rough country.

But once when he was bringing some brood mares
down from the hills he got onto a salt flat.
He let the other horses go on ahead and then
took off after them.

That horse could really run on level ground, he said.
The wind made tears come to your eyes.

got drunk once with another cowpuncher
named Roscoe Knipp. They were in Boulder,
Colorado, and it was Prohibition and Roscoe
knew where to go.

They drank two or three kinds of rotgut
whiskey.

In the middle of the night he woke up and
crawled out to a stream that was running
by their campsite and drank till he
was full.

The next morning he felt fine.

He

was never called Wild Bill
or Big Bad Bill,
just Bill.

And sometimes
Willie.

He

used to climb trees that were
over a hundred feet high. But not
for fun. He was chasing a squirrel
down so his dog could get it.

"What'd you do with a squirrel once you caught it?"
"Why, we ate it."
"Didn't the dog eat it himself?"
"Not enough to speak of."

He

bought a three-bedroom house in 1948 so that
my mother's mother would always have a place.

She stayed with us eleven months and then
went back to the farm.

Not long ago he finished paying it off.
The taxes are six times what they were.

He

told me that I shouldn't have books like that
in the house. He meant *Fever Heat,* a paperback
about stock car racing.

It always fell open to the page where Ace Martin
seduces the young widow who has lost her husband
in a fiery crash.

The best part used the words *breast* and *cleave*.
It used the first one twice.

He

was looking for work at 47 and the owner of a
new concrete-coring plant down in the valley
finally came out and told him that he was
too old.

He

was taken out of school after
the eighth grade.

He put me through eighteen grades.
And then some.

He

has never written me a letter himself.
Or called.

My mother dials and says,
"Here he is."

He

drove a school bus for the extra money.
At Christmas he gave everybody some little
gift.

He got 17 Ace combs, 6 Scripto pencils and
hundreds of cookies.

gave me 50 dollars for Christmas one year, and when I came back from the trotters at Fairmont Park and said that I'd dropped 20 it made him mad.

But he never said anything.

He

used to do most everything himself
but now that he's retired
he talks about experts and professionals.
He said that a professional would have to come
and trim the hundred-foot elm in the front yard,
that it would take an expert to adjust the
carburetor on the power mower.

He

has a new double-knit suit with slightly flared
pants. The salesman at Robert Hall told him that
he could sleep in it or throw it in the corner like
a rag and it wouldn't wrinkle,

but

he should be careful not to snag it because it was
next to impossible to mend and he should not smoke
in it because it might catch on fire.

He

gave me his car
again
so that I could take Cherry on a little
nostalgia trip. After the hometown,
her old friends, houses where she
used to live and a few schools

we'd stop at a cemetery outside New Berlin
where her grandmother is buried.

Talking on the phone to someone I heard
him say that we were going North for
a few days, up there where there were
graveyards
and things.

He

walked in the basement all winter. For exercise.
Outside the cold air bothered his angina. He could
not get 100 yards, even with a grey Styrofoam mask
that covered his nose and mouth and warmed the air.

In April they went to a funeral, the father of a man
neither one of them had seen in years.

Later my mother called to say that although the tulips
were up and the sun was shining he was still downstairs.
She believed it was because he was afraid he'd fall
in the street.

About that time he came to the phone and said that he
thought he probably felt a little better
than usual.

said, "What the devil!" when he dropped
a 75-pound can of ice cream on his foot.

I only heard this story once after I'd
begun to swear

and then not from him.

once owned a blind horse, a big gray who
worked well in harness and trusted his rider,
"If he was trustworthy to begin with."

Two cousins, 12 and 10, were coming to stay
at the farm for a while, so he took the horse
to Harrisburg where there was a community
sale. He was going to trade so the boys
would have something to gallop.

The auctioneer began by saying that here was
a fine saddle horse that knew every gait
under the sun.

The bidding started at
fifteen dollars.

lies on the same couch that he used to
only sit on, straight up as if the newsmen
might ask him to spring into action.

He used to work twelve hours of the day making
ice cream from scratch. Then home, charging
around the lawn. Grass that had been mashed
flat he brought to attention then cut if off
at the roots, snuffing it out,
heartless.

He took one vacation, looking at the water in
Michigan with one eye, turning at every little
thing, each sound a customer. We dined at
roadside stands, covering six states in a week.
He ate standing, like a man on the run.

I saw him again last summer, four months past a
coronary. He rested in bed, gathering strength
for a nap, hands behind his head,
eyes full of ceilings.

PRONOUNCING MY NAME

When someone leans in and says, "Koohurch?
Curcheese? Curgoo?" I just nod. Believe
me, it's easier.

When someone wipes his brow and asks, "What
the hell kind of name is that, anyway?" I
say that it's probably German. Like Goethe.

Whom I used to refer to casually as, in high
school, I also let it be known that my great
great grandparents, being modest immigrants,
had simply dropped the title Von. Actually
I was an aristocrat. Sure, Ronald Von Koertge
The Twerp.

"Coeur," said Robert one day. "Maybe it's French."
Could it be Ronald Heart, like in sweetheart?
How wonderful. What did the Germans invent, anyway,
but anal retentiveness.

But the French, they drink wine all the time
and think nudity is okay. Now I can stop
worrying that I would have looked good in a long
leather coat. I have a great new hometown, France.
Where, by the way, my great great great great
grandfather invented the sweetest kiss of them all.

remember the teacher who inspired them to great leaps of
    learning
I remember the one who had all the ugly girls after him.
Jesus, he was a nice guy: every day they sat in the back
    row
with their tubs of No-Blem and every day after class he
    would
stand in the hall and answer question after dumb question.

In a frenzy of high-mindedness and Christian calculation I
    resolved
that if I was ever in a similar position, I would do as he
    did.

The eighties is not the decade for it: all the girls seem to
    know the
score. The ugly ones now have ugly boyfriends and the
    pretty ones
are seen with the football team and the band.

Where were you, Brunhilde, Helga and Olive? I thought
    we were supposed
to meet under the clock.

My only love reads big books, behemoth works
of unassigned origin: *War and Peace, The
Rise and Fall of the Third Reich,* Gaddis'
The Recognitions and gloomy Spengler.

She only tackles these monsters when things
go wrong upstairs: her childlessness, my
childishness. Usually in the mornings, some
time between the bran flakes and the mail,

I hear her groan of exertion, a wheeze of
heft, howl of upholstery, whoosh of the page
and I know her blood is running grim and
this is no place for a kid like me.

was my bones. As I gave them
to her one at a time she put
them in a bag from Saks.

As long as I didn't hesitate
she collected scapula and
vertebrae with a smile.

If I grew reluctant she pouted.
Then I would come across with
rib cage or pelvis.

Eventually I lay in a puddle
at her feet, only the boneless
penis waving like an anemone.

"Look at yourself," she said.
"You're disgusting."

The Ubiquity of
the Need for Love

I leave the number and a short
message on every green Volvo
in town

> Is anything wrong?
> I miss you.
> 574-7423

The phone rings constantly.
One says, Are you bald?
Another, How tall are you in
your stocking feet?

Most just reply, Nothing's wrong.
I miss you, too.

Come quick.

I Wanted My Name on the Side
of a Building
I Wanted to be as Feared as the Word
Biopsy

But women pass as if I were a urinal.
I have a watch as big as a pie, nobody
even asks.

I go into a bar and give some customer
a profile and a half. He peers into
his beer.

I spit into his glass. Now he speaks
up and the bartender reaches for
a club. Their distaste is like
soothing hands at my brow.

Some girls are in a booth; my eyes
are open sesames but they do not enter.
I go over and show them my
dossier. They retreat and thugs
rise from the dim leather like stumps
in drought.

The cops come in wearing pieces
of the sky. They take me out like
an octopus. People line the sidewalk,
wishing for cameras.

Tonight they will pass my name around
the table like
steak.

She comes home steaming.
She gets into my pants.
She rides me hard.

I look past her slot
machine eyes
to the ceiling

where the 1969 earthquake
made cracks in the shape
of Florida

and Louisiana, the latter
having for its capital
Baton Rouge,

which is located on the Mississippi River,
principal waterway
of the United States,

measuring 2470 miles
from its source in
Northern Minnesota
to the Gulf of Mexico.

Every now and then we went out to dinner and afterwards parked somewhere until she stopped me.

I kind of liked that. I haven't been stopped in years, not because I'm anything special but because I live in California and it gets dark.

We did this for about six months, from just after Christmas until right around my birthday.

And every time I called I said, "Koertge, Ron Koertge."

I go everywhere underground. It is a burden I have
imposed on myself: I want to deserve her love.

Accordingly when she goes out, I begin to dig; the
tap of her heels on the pavement drives me on.

Occasionally I come to the surface behind the gas
station and pass her on the street. "Hi, there!"
She never nods, which is as it should be since

she does not know who I am or that—for her—
I live to burrow or how at night, curled in the
end of my present tunnel, I think about her

pretty feet and giggle in the rooty air and
go to sleep.

Her conversation is interminable.
Throughout it she looks about brightly.
At intervals she faces each important
Direction. No doubt she informs her

Party that she is standing in a
Nearly invisible booth; she marvels.
Then leaves and I move to her cubicle.
Ah! It is she. I hold the warm plastic

To my cheek. The perforations are briny.
I suck at her warm cigarette. I
Pocket a Kleenex. I inhale once, twice:
Hold. Her stink reels me, reels me.

Tap! What? Tap, tap. I am wary. I turn,
A casual caller. A female in the next
Compartment leans toward the glass, plants
Her open mouth there. She tilts

Her head, urges her lips apart. I see her
Tongue, a slug, on the glass. I come to it
Like a connoisseur. Then we retire, straighten,
Feel for coins and leave, each in his own way.

Getting the License

I am causing a sensation here in the County Clerk's
    crummy
office, but it is only because I am not wearing Hush
    Puppies
like my colleagues in near-groomdom. Yes, that must
    be it,

there is nothing else it could be: the prancing
    Arabian stands
docile at the curb, the ocelot lies quietly at my booted
    feet,
the canaries and kingfishers are active but not noisy.
    I wonder

if it can be the salamander? I do not think so, that
    man
over there has one also, or is that his tie? No time for
conjecture now, they require our signatures. My
    child bride

looks up at me as we swear the information given
    above is the
truth and the whole truth. I give my love a ruby for
    her smile,
hand the unmarried clerk a check for a zillion dollars
    and

shake hands all around. In each eager palm I leave a
    coin, a
gold doubloon still cold and wet from the sea. Outside
    the crowd
Ahhhhhs as I throw her across the saddle. The
    steed whirls once,

twice and suddenly rises into the air. As we float into the

evening sky a million children light their matches and her name

appears in flame across a hundred square miles of wilderness. She

looks down at the speeding earth. "Yes," she says, "Of course,

but do you love me? Do you really, *really* love me?" What a

girl! I lean forward, spurring the horse to incredible heights.

As the galaxies spin themselves out behind us, I call to her,

"Look," I shout. "Look at this." I rise in my stirrups and—

because she wisely prefers gesture to emotion— I eat the moon.

Whippersnappers

On raw days Cherry stands at the back door and
watches his tailored wife care for her plant
while I look out the front where Arnie in an
old football jersey washes his car.

It is between rounds. Still back to back like
injured parties, we wish for more money, bigger
biceps or breasts, a dinner to go to, one clean
glass, children and other ceremonies.

Then somebody breaks something else and nobody
cleans that up, either. I go out and stay out.
Or she does.

Sometimes Cherry naps and I sit in the sun on
my sleepy dune-colored Dodge and nurse Schlitz
while Arnie buffs his red Ford that has a hole
in the hood so the engine can stick out.

Arnie has told me some amazing things.
Last month: he made a list of friends and
stopped at 500. Last week: he has never argued
with Joyce, never cheated on her, never will.
Today: thirteen months from now he will get
his master's and settle down: Gregory & Son.

He looks at the foothills, the reverent sponge
hesitates. I can see the future in his eyes and
it is arranged like the furniture of his spotless
house.

Indoors I look through the rubble for Cherry. When
I wake her she says, "Anything wrong?" And I answer
"No. Move over."

Last–Minute Change of Plans

Cherry and I were going up the clubhouse elevator
when she said, "Boy, I could find you anywhere
in the world."
"How's that?" I ask idly, keeping my nose in a tough
grass race for fillies and mares.
"I'd just go to the nearest track."
"What nearest track."
"Fairmont down the hill from your folks' house.
Or the one in Tucson. Or Centennial, you liked
Denver."
"Tracks are big places. You'd never catch me."
"Ha. You always go to the paddock. I'd just hang
around there. You'd show up."

She studied Spanish while I messed around with deuces
till there was a race I could bet. Now and then
I would look over and smile, but I was thinking
about sweet Julie in white shorts packing and,
at this very moment, writing a note to her
dumbfounded parents.

"These Students Couldn't Write
Their Way out of a Paper Bag"
—Anonymous

I gather groups of freshmen. I distribute
blue books and pens, then unveil the bag
big as a bus.

They rush in and I twist the opening.
There is much classified argot, many
contempo shibboleths but, sure enough,
nobody is writing his way out.

Still, the bag is moving rhythmically.
There are unified, coherent and adequately
developed moans. Whatever they are doing
has a beginning, middle and end.

"I want to give you all A's." I shout
as the bag develops an afterglow and
damp spots appear all over the place.

It's me or a book report and they are taking
notes for Lit. What did the Poet Read? What
Were His Themes? What Are The Main Differences
Between This Poet And Your Lunch Hour? Explain.

She is late for the reading and she is beautiful.
Heads move like fight fans keeping track
of her perilous shorts and the whole promise
of folly she wears like a towel.

I answer questions about McKuen, about rough
drafts. I get my fifty bucks.

"I don't see how you do it," says the paymaster
and advisor to the school magazine.

"Fifty dollars is a lot of money to me."

"I can't even send out manuscripts because
the rejections hurt too much."

"It's the money, that's all."

"They were more interested in that girl than
in what you had to say."

"A dollar a minute is pretty good money."

"I just don't see how you do it. I mean,
they don't even listen."

was always old, so when I saw her at the nursing
home she just seemed more
faint.

She was balsa in a white gown, stained at the
center. She called me Bill and my father
answered.

When she slept she moved her feet like a lifer.
Awake, she roamed the past, a historian.

My father and I looked at each other, shook our
heads, watched tv.

It was football season; the game was half done.
On the field in Stetsons and tasseled boots
cowgirls from Dallas showed their silken
crotches to the world.

Going home we were on a two-lane suicide road.
He was driving fast through dark as thick as
earth. "That wasn't her," he said, putting
his right hand over his heart like a man
at a parade.

of the hospital with the news that
my daughter has a skull like
marmalade
and may, at fifteen, learn to talk

like a fish

I look in the window of the store by
the bus stop and see myself
collar open
tousled hair

and

I think that in another day or two
when the smudges under my eyes are
even darker

I will be very, very attractive

indeed.

Sunday

Everybody is all dressed up this morning, everybody that
    is
but me.
I do not think I will find myself in the rotogravure
whatever that is
and if I do
I will be pictured as Before.

All the Afters in the world are walking around with their
children
named Kirsten and Shannon and Kent:
wimples are nodding to bonnets
nobody is picking his nose
there is not an open fly in town.

And here I sit with last night's soup still in my
mustache.
No creative thinking here, folks, not a
dynamic angle
in the whole room.

My newest wife is standing in the
decaying kitchen truly saddened by the death of a
black and white cat
who ate all his meals here. The phone rings but
she does not move a muscle.
We both know it is just another threat from
Betty Crocker.

It is the thirteenth Sunday of
a short year
and as I look out the window at the people going by
I wonder
If Jesus yawned or anything that morning
and
if he really wanted to go back outside
at all.

She often lies with her hands behind her head
in a San Quentin pose, arms forming a pair
of small empty wings.

She does not slip from the bath in a loose
towel, according Follies' glimpses
of rump and thigh. She does lumber by
in a robe of immense dunciness.

Her dates are fixed up or blind
often, like specimens, behind thick glass.
She leaves late, returns by twelve, afraid
perhaps that she will turn into
something worse.

She comes to me and wants to know what to do.
I say I do not know.
She comes to me and wants to know if it will
ever be all right.
I say Yes but it will take a long time.

Night Games

The announcer sets the stage
as I do dishes:

a green lawn reflects into
the upper deck. The clean-up
man taps his spikes

and I reach for the big green
bowl as he belts one over
the scoreboard breaking a
wineglass.

I turn off the faucet
just in time, saving 32,000
people from drowning.

Sleep

Boy, is it crowded here in the arms of Morpheus.
I wish I were a little closer to that girl over
there in the knee socks and Saint Mary of Sorrows
plaid skirt, though she has brought her bicycle
seat to bed with her so it will be safe from
men like me.

I am too tired for little Rose Ann, anyway. It
is all I can do to hold onto my capital Z. My
arms are as heavy as Kong's, everyone's are.
Yet just before sleep we fling our letters
into the air where they arrange themselves
into the sound of woodsmen.

While sitting home one warm night, I hear the burglars
    fiddling
with the lock. This is what I have been waiting for.

I run around to the back and open the door, invite them in
    and
pour some drinks. I tell them to be comfortable and help
    them
off with shoes and masks.

In a little while we are fast friends, and after a dozen toasts
to J. Edgar Hoover they begin to carry things out. I point to
the hidden silver, hold the door as they wrestle with the
    bed
and generally make myself useful.

Then when the truck is loaded and they come back inside
    for one
last look, I get the drop on them. Using Spike's gun I shoot
them both and imprint Blackie's prints on the handle.

Then I get in the van and drive away,
a happy man.